Three-Dimensional Embroidery Stitches

To my daughter, Maria.

Three-Dimensional Embroidery Stitches

Pat Trott

SEARCH PRESS

First published in Great Britain 2005

Search Press Limited
Wellwood, North Farm Road,
Tunbridge Wells, Kent TN2 3DR

Reprinted 2006

ISBN 1 84448 003 8

The Publishers and author can accept no responsibility for any
consequences arising from the information, advice or instructions
given in this publication.

Readers are permitted to reproduce any of the items/patterns in
this book for their personal use, or for the purposes of selling for
charity, free of charge and without the prior permission of the
Publishers. Any use of the items/patterns for commercial purposes
is not permitted without the prior permission of the Publishers.

Suppliers
If you have difficulty in obtaining any of the materials and
equipment mentioned in this book, then please write to the
Publishers, at the address above, for a current list of stockists,
including firms who operate a mail-order service.

Publisher's note
All the step-by-step photographs in this book feature the
author, Pat Trott, demonstrating three-dimensional
embroidery stitches. No models have been used.

Acknowledgements
*I would like to thank everyone at Search Press, especially
Sophie, for their gentle guidance, support, encouragement
and forbearance.*

*My grateful thanks to my son-in-law, Richard, who is always
willing to make frames of any size I ask for,
uncomplainingly and immediately.*

*A big thank you to Sarah-Jane and Jane at Threads of
Amersham for their friendship and helpfulness and for
generously supplying fabric and threads.*

*Last, but certainly not least, a very big thank you to all my
friends, especially Annie, for their continuing interest,
support and generous help over the years. They keep me
going when things get tough.*

Page 1 The stone wall was created from pieces of vilene covered in stocking fabric. The moss between the stones was worked in couched bouclé. The gate is raised stem band and the tree was made with twisted thread couched down. The meadow was worked in a combination of velvet stitch for the green areas and tufting for other colours. Pages 2–3 The owl's eyes are French knots, the top of his head was worked in whipped spider's web and each of his feathers are woven picots. His legs are worked in raised chain band and his claws are bullion knots. The petals for most of the flowers were worked in long curved bullion knots but some are curved cast on buttonholes. The flower centres were made with a combination of French knots and tufting. The stems were worked in Portuguese knotted stem stitch and each leaf is raised leaf stitch worked over card. Above: Two beautiful tablecloths embroidered by my mother. Page 5 This design is an array of whipped spider's webs, some with open centres. Pages 6–7 This Celtic rainbow comprises seven rows of raised chain band.

Contents

Introduction

As a traditional hand embroiderer I love stitches. I am never happier than when I have a needle and thread in my hand. I love executing stitches and seeing what they look like and how I can use them to represent my ideas.

My mother was an embroiderer and, like many of you, I was brought up to embroider household items such as cushion covers, table mats and tablecloths. When I married and had my children, time was in very short supply and I enrolled in an evening class so that for two hours, once a week, I could embroider. It was during that evening class that I found a whole new world of techniques and stitches. It led to other classes, residential weekends and attendance at many exhibitions. I joined the Embroiderers' Guild and took City & Guilds courses in embroidery and teaching embroidery of all kinds.

Whilst exploring the many stitches available I found some that did not lie flat on the surface, but stood away from the fabric giving the embroidery a textured and three-dimensional look. I would like to share these exciting stitches with you so that you can give your embroidery another dimension. I will start by showing you how these stitches are executed, then show you how to put them together to represent many different images. When you use these stitches to create the illusion of flowers, you have to have stems to attach them to, so I have also included some flatter stitches that you can use for the stems. I will also show you some other techniques to combine with these stitches to enable you to produce an exciting and beautiful piece of work.

Hand embroidery is a slow process, so allow yourself the luxury of a little time just for you. Gather together a variety of colourful threads, some fabric, a frame, needle and scissors, find a comfortable chair and enjoy the journey. Have fun and happy stitching.

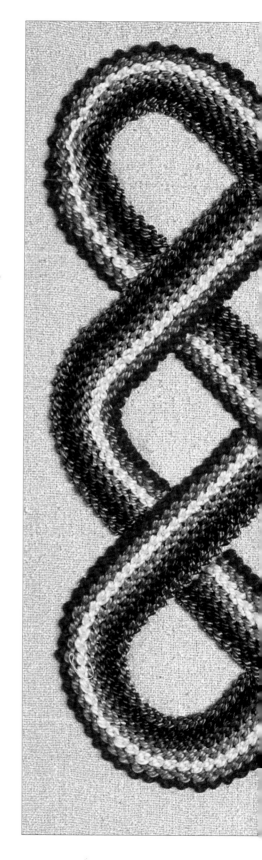

Materials

Fabric

Surface embroidery requires a closely woven fabric. I have used silk noil for all the embroideries in this book. This can be obtained from specialist embroidery shops. I like working on this fabric as it is lovely and soft and the needle and thread seems to slide through it easily. Also it is not 'flat' and has a slightly textured look and feel. It comes in a fine and medium thickness. I have used the heaviest of these. I have used a fine calico as a backing.

If you cannot obtain silk noil, you could use a medium weight calico instead. This is very easily obtainable from embroidery or haberdashery shops. This can also be backed with a fine calico.

Make sure you buy enough fabric to allow for mounting on to a frame while working, and also to leave enough room from the edge of your embroidery to the edge of the finished item for framing when completed.

Left to right: Silk noil, medium calico and fine calico.

Threads

Stranded cotton is probably the thread you are most familiar with, and it is the most easily obtainable. It comes in a skein and in a wide variety of colours. Each length that you pull from the skein is made up of six separate threads. You can use these in any multiple from one strand on its own, up to all six together.

Perlé cotton is easy to use and very amenable. It is readily available in a wide variety of colours and in four thicknesses: 3, 5, 8 and 12; 3 being the thickest and 12 being the finest. It is a single, twisted, mercerised cotton thread and comes in skeins and balls.

Coton à broder is also a single, twisted, mercerised cotton thread. It has a slightly softer twist than perlé, and is lovely to use. It comes in a wide variety of colours, but limited thicknesses.

Embroidery soft comes in just one thickness and is a matte cotton, but it does come in lots of beautiful colours and is ideal for making large French knots.

There are are also many lovely threads that can be found in specialist embroidery shops:

Bouclé is a crinkly, textured thread and can come in one plain colour or be space-dyed, which means it has been dyed randomly so that there are a myriad of colours in one skein. It is ideal for couching as moss, or for a mass of flowers.

Chenille is a soft, fluffy thread that is best used for couching where you want a textured, knobbly look, such as bark on a tree trunk. Like bouclé, it can come in one colour or be space-dyed.

Silk is available in many different thicknesses and colours.

Variegated textured thread comes in skeins. Each skein contains a variety of threads in different types, thicknesses, textures and shades of colour.

Have fun looking through catalogues and visiting specialist embroidery shops and purchase a variety of threads so that you have a goody bag to dip into.

Variegated textured thread in skeins. This is available in many colours.

Clockwise from middle top: stranded cotton, bouclé, coton à broder, perlé 3, embroidery soft, perlé 5, home-dyed silk yarn, bought space-dyed 3 ply cotton, chenille and in the middle perlé 8.

9

Needles

I use a variety of different types of needles according to the stitches I am working. You will find that what you need will also depend on the thickness of the thread you are working with. Always choose a needle with an eye large enough to thread easily.

Chenille needles come in sizes 18 to 24. They have larger eyes than crewel needles and are slightly thicker.

Crewel needles are finer than chenille needles and come in sizes 4 to 10. Both of these needles have a sharp point.

Tapestry needles have a blunt point and a long eye. They come in sizes 18 to 26 and are ideal to use for woven picots and spider's web.

Betweens are also known as quilting needles. They are fine and small, ideal for couching down a thick thread with a fine thread. Useful sizes are 10 and 12.

I use a long **darning needle** for making bullion knots and cast on buttonholes. Pick one with an eye large enough to take the thread that you are using.

A **milliner's needle** is similar to a long darning needle, but has a smaller and thinner eye. This needle is the same thickness all the way along, so it is easier to use for bullion knots and cast on buttonholes.

Doll needles are usually used by soft toy enthusiasts but I use them for making long woven picots when a pin is just not long enough. Doll needles come in lengths of 89mm (3½in), 130mm (5in) and 174mm (7in).

Long, glass-headed pin This is used to make woven picots.

My needle case showing some of the needles that I used to execute the embroideries in this book, and a long, glass-headed pin.

Padding

Stocking nylon can be used for creating the effect of stones, rocks and pebbles. It can be stuffed with wadding to make round stones or stretched over pieces of craft vilene to make flat paving stones.

Wadding is a commercially produced fabric that can be used to stuff stocking nylon to make stone effects.

Craft vilene is a dense, felt-like fabric that is easy to cut into small pieces.

Craft vilene, wadding, stocking nylon and shapes cut from craft vilene.

Fabric decoration

To avoid 'blank page syndrome' and to give my embroideries depth, I paint a wash on to the fabric before I start stitching. This wash can be achieved with fabric paints or with water soluble crayons or pencils and is explained more fully in the Colouring fabric section on pages 41–42.

The picture below shows a variety of colouring media together with the brushes and natural sponge used to apply the colour to the fabric.

Brushes, water soluble crayons and pencils, fabric paints, a water dish and a natural sponge.

Work station

I like my working frame to be held in a stand. There are a variety of stands available. I have a metal Lowery stand. It consists of a footplate that slots under your chair to keep it stable and an adjustable arm attached to a pole. A clamp on the end of the arm grips your frame. Levers on the height pole and arm allow you to position your frame at the most comfortable height and angle. Loosening the arm lever also allows you to turn the frame right over to finish off and start new threads, without taking the frame off the stand.

Good light is essential when you are stitching. If you are lucky enough to have time to embroider during the day, you can sit near a window, but if you can only grab an hour or two during the evenings, an anglepoise lamp fitted with a daylight or halogen bulb is a very good substitute. I am right-handed, so I have my light source coming over my left shoulder, so that as I stitch, my right hand does not cast a shadow on the area I am stitching. Of course, if you are left-handed, your light source will need to come from the right-hand side. If you sit facing a table, the light can come from the front facing you. I find that a good light is better than magnification.

It is important to be comfortable, so make sure that you have your threads, scissors, needles and any other items to hand before you begin. Once you are comfy, start stitching!

My Lowery stand. The thread holder means that I can hang out my selection of threads for the project and have them near to hand while working.

My anglepoise lamp, fitted with a daylight bulb because I rarely get time to do embroidery during the day.

Other items

Home-made frame My son-in-law makes me wooden frames, like picture frames, to the sizes I need. They are made from lengths of soft wood, mitred at the corners and then glued and stapled together.

Staple gun This is used to staple fabric to a home-made frame.

Seat frame It is an advantage to have both hands free when stitching. A seat frame enables you to do this, as it has a flat 'foot' that can be placed under your leg to keep it steady while you are stitching.

Tambour, ring or round frame These are available in a variety of sizes from 7.5cm (3in) to 30.5cm (12in) in diameter. Each frame consists of two wooden rings that fit inside one another. The outer ring has an adjustable screw to enable you to tighten it around the inner ring and this keeps the fabric taut. The inner ring should be bound with **bias binding** or tape. This helps to prevent marking the fabric and also helps to keep it taut.

Scissors You need two pairs: dressmaking shears to cut the fabric and embroidery scissors to cut the thread.

Water soluble marker pen This is used to draw the lines of your design on the fabric. It is removed with a paintbrush dipped in cold water once you have finished your project. Test it before use by making a mark on the edge of your fabric. Try to remove it using a damp paintbrush. If it comes out easily, go ahead and mark out all the design. Do not iron the pen marks as this will fix them. Be careful not to use an air soluble pen, as the marks will disappear in air, often before you have time to finish the project!

Card Small pieces of card are used for the raised leaf stitch.

Drawing pins/silk pins These can be used instead of staples to attach the fabric to a home-made frame.

Screwdriver This is used to tighten the screw on a tambour frame and to loosen the staples in a home-made frame when you have finished the embroidery.

Pliers These are used to remove the staples from the frame after you have loosened them as above.

Tape measure This is used to measure the fabric before cutting. Remember that you need to allow for excess fabric around the edge of the planned design so that you can attach it to a frame.

Toothbrush This is used to fluff up the cuts threads in velvet stitch.

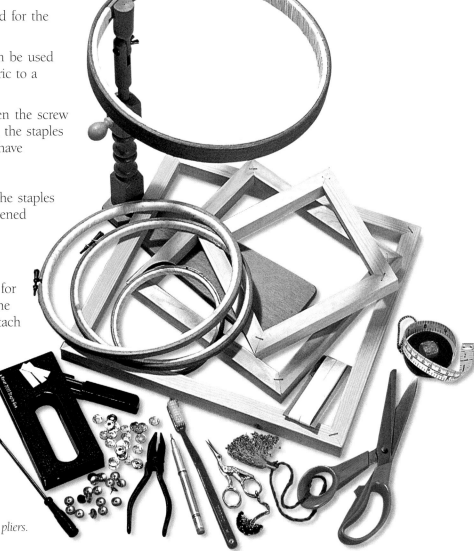

Clockwise from bottom left: a screwdriver, drawing pins and silk pins, staple gun, bits of card used in some stitches, home-made frames, tambour frames, a seat frame, bias binding, tape measure, dressmaking scissors, embroidery scissors, toothbrush, water soluble pen and pliers.

13

Stitches

This book contains seventeen stitches. The step by step photographs show you how to execute the stitches and the Sampler on pages 36–39 shows how I have used them to create the illusion of flowers. The stitches can also be used in other ways, as shown in the embroideries on the cover and in the early pages of the book. Use a sharp needle, such as a chenille, for each stitch unless otherwise specified. The size of needle that you choose will depend on the thickness of the thread that you are using.

Stem stitch

Stem stitch is a line stitch which makes it particularly good for stems or branches. The finished effect should look like a rope. It looks best used for straight lines, or slightly curved lines, but does not work well on very tight curves or circles. Work from the bottom of a line up towards the top, away from you. The length of the stitches you make will depend on the thickness of the thread. When using a fine thread, make the stitches small and when using a thicker thread, make them longer.

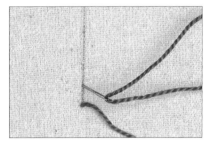

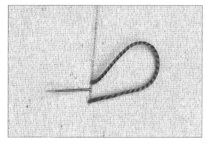

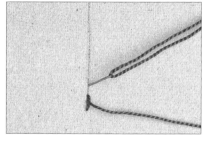

1. Come up from the back at the bottom of the line and go down a little way up the line, keeping the thread to the right of the needle.

2. Come up again half way between where you came up last and where you went down, keeping the thread on the right. Pull the thread through. Steps 1 and 2 apply to the first stitch only.

3. Keep the thread to the right, then go back down again a little further up the line.

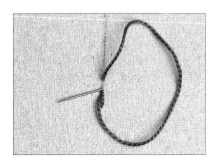

4. Bring the needle and thread up through the same hole as the top of the first stitch. Repeat steps 3 and 4 to complete the line of stitches.

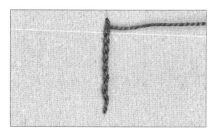

A finished line of stem stitches.

Palestrina knot stitch

This is a beautiful, textured line stitch that can be used for stems or branches that need a knobbly look. It is also known as double knot stitch. I like the knots to be quite close together, but you can place them further apart if you want to. Once started, you will get into a good rhythm and find that it is a particularly soothing stitch to do. It looks best in a thick thread and is worked from top to bottom down the line.

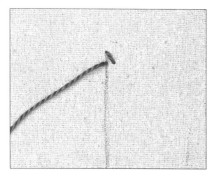

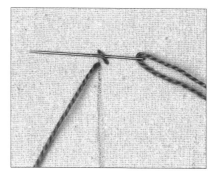

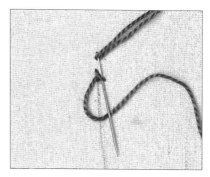

1. Come out at the top of the line and go down just below and slightly to the right, to form a small diagonal stitch. Come up on the line again, level with the bottom of the diagonal stitch and below the first point where you came up. Keep the thread down towards you, out of the way, and to the left.

2. Pass the needle from right to left under the diagonal stitch to make the first wrap.

3. Make an anticlockwise circle with the thread, then pass the needle from top to bottom under the diagonal stitch, making sure that the thread is under the needle. Pull the thread taut towards you in a straight line to make a knot.

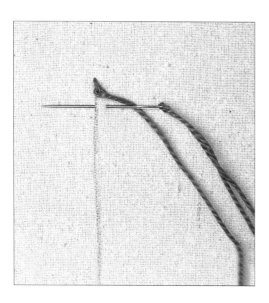

4. Go down to the right of the line and then back up on the line to make another diagonal stitch. Repeat steps 2, 3 and 4 until the line of knots is the length you want.

A line of Palestrina knot stitches worked.

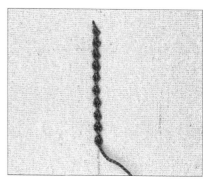

Portuguese knotted stem stitch

This stitch is ideal for creating a slighter thicker line than stem stitch can give you. It is also very useful when you need a textured stem or branch. It is worked away from you, from the bottom of the line up towards the top. You will soon get into the rhythm of the stitch and find it very therapeutic and soothing, it looks more complicated than it is!

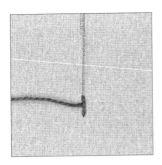

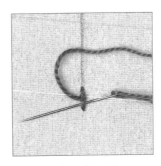
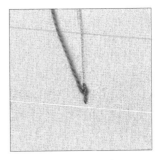

1. Come up at the bottom of the line, go down a little way above it, keeping the thread to the right of the needle (not shown) and come up again half way between where you came up and went down (as with stem stitch).

2. You now need to wrap this stitch twice. Keep the thread to the left, and pass the needle from right to left under the stitch and below the working thread. This is wrap one.

3. Pull the thread through to complete the first wrap, then repeat this move, making sure the second wrap is below the first.

4. Pull the thread upwards and slightly to the left to make sure the two wraps tighten and are together in a little knot. Steps 1 to 4 are done only once to get the stitch started.

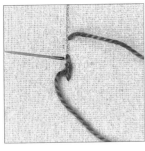

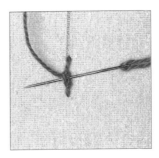
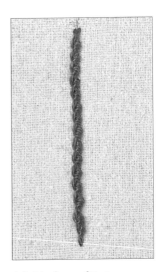

5. Go down above the previous stitch. Come up level with the top of the previous stitch, just to its left, keeping the working thread to the right of the needle. The bottom of the new stitch should overlap the top of the previous stitch.

6. Pass the needle under the two overlapping threads from right to left and pull taut. This is the first wrap on your second stitch.

7. Pass the needle under the two overlapping threads from right to left again, below the first wrap. Pull taut again. This is the second wrap on your second stitch.

A finished row of Portuguese knotted stem stitch. Steps 5 to 7 were repeated to complete the line.

French knots

French knots should look like an old-fashioned 'bun' hairstyle – nice and round with a dimple in the middle. To achieve this effect, you should only wrap the thread round the needle once. To make knots of different sizes, you should vary the thickness of thread that you use rather than vary the number of wraps. If you want a small French knot, use a fine thread and if you want a large knot then use a thick thread such as embroidery soft.

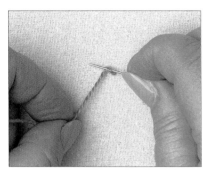

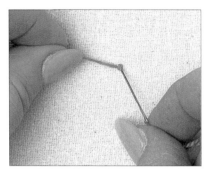

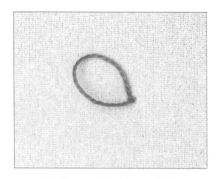

1. Come up from the back where you want the knot to be. Hold the thread in your left hand, put the needle on top of the thread and wrap the thread round it once.

2. Go back down into the fabric very close to where you came out. When the needle is halfway through the fabric, gently pull the thread tight round the needle. Be careful not to go down into the same hole or the knot will go through the fabric to the back and you will lose it.

3. Pull the needle through the fabric to form a nice, neat circle with a dimple in the middle. This picture shows the knot before the thread is pulled right through.

A cluster of finished French knots.

Tufting

This is a quick and easy way of using little tufts of threads to represent flowers in the distance, or in a field, or places where you want just a hint of a flower. For instance, if you use red thread, a small tuft would represent a poppy, yellow could be a dandelion or buttercup, blue could be a cornflower and white could be a daisy. Tufts are made with stranded cotton. When you pull a length from a skein, the strands are usually twisted round each other. This stitch requires that you separate the strands and then put them back together so that they are smooth and untwisted. Use a crewel or chenille needle, with a large eye, for this stitch.

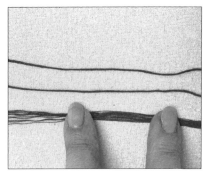

1. Separate twelve strands of stranded cotton, then put them back together and smooth them so they are not twisted together.

2. Go down through the fabric from the front to the back.

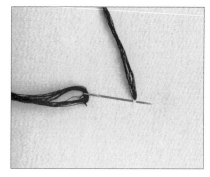

3. Turn to the back of your work and, holding on to the strands at the front, make a very small holding stitch in the backing fabric to secure the threads, so that you cannot pull them right through the fabric.

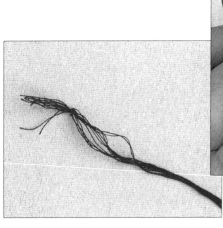

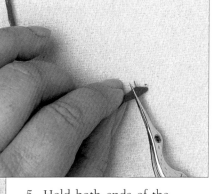

4. Turn to the front of your work and pull the needle back to the front very close to where you went down.

5. Hold both ends of the working thread together and cut them short to make a little tuft.

A cluster of finished tufts.

Woven picot

This is a very versatile, free-standing stitch, shown to me many years ago by the embroiderer Muriel Best. You can make it short and fat, long and thin or anything in between. It is best executed in a single twisted thread such as perlé or coton à broder. Use a blunt tapestry needle so that you do not split the threads. It can be used for petals, sepals, leaves or feathers and I am sure that once you have mastered it, you will find many more uses for it. I used it for the feathers on the owl on page 2. If you use it in rows, as on the owl, start on the bottom row of your design and work up to the top, so that each row overlaps the previous row.

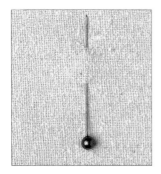

1. Put a pin in the fabric as shown. The distance between the entry point and the exit point will determine the length of the picot.

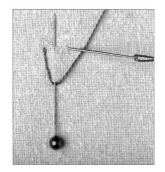

2. Come up on the left-hand side of the pin, level with where it exits the fabric. Take the thread around the pin head and go down on the right, level with the starting point, leaving a slightly wider gap on the right-hand side. The distance between where you came up and where you went down determines the width of the picot.

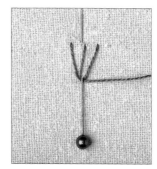

3. Come up close to and just to the right of the pin, level with the other two threads. Take the thread round the pin head again, left to right, to make three spokes.

4. Going from right to left, take the needle and thread under the right-hand spoke, over the middle spoke and under the left-hand spoke. This traps the middle thread in place.

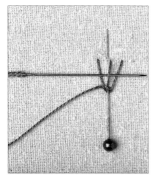

5. Next go from left to right, over, under and over the spokes.

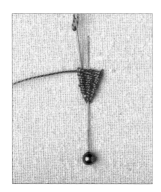

6. Keep weaving from side to side. Take care not to pull the sides in, but pack the rows up as tightly as you can. When you cannot put any more rows in, take your needle round the last spoke to the back of the fabric.

When you pull the pin out, the woven picot leaf or petal will stand up from the fabric.

19

Raised cup stitch

In this stitch rows of knots are built up one on top of the other to create, as the name implies, a little cup. It is best executed in a single twisted thread such as perlé or coton à broder. Multiples of thread do not seem to work as you cannot see the construction of the stitch easily. Use a needle with a blunt point such as a tapestry needle.

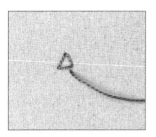

1. Make a triangle of small straight stitches then come up on the outside of this triangle at one corner. You will be working clockwise.

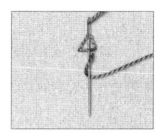

2. Put the needle from the inside to the outside, under the bottom stitch of the triangle and to the left of the emerging thread. Wrap the thread over and under the needle as shown.

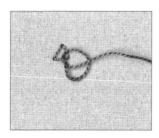

3. Pull the needle and thread towards you to form a knot on the bottom stitch of the triangle.

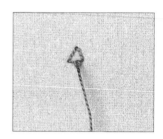

4. The first knot pulled tight. Make another knot next to it in the same way.

5. Make two knots on each side of the triangle. When you have done this and gone all the way around the triangle and come back to the start, you will see there is a small length of thread between the point where the working thread comes out of the fabric and the first knot on the first side. This is where you join up to start the second row of knots. Take your needle under this first piece of thread and make another knot to join your stitches into a circle.

6. The second row of knots is made in the gaps between the knots on the first row. There will be a gap between the two knots on each side and a gap across each corner. Make the knots for your second row in these gaps (see diagram, left). Keep adding rows in this way until the cup is the height you desire.

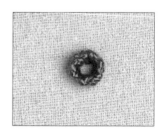

When it is the required height, very carefully weave the thread down the outside of the cup, take it through to the back of the fabric and finish off. Take care not to pull tightly or you will pull your cup out of shape.

Whipped spider's web

This is an easy stitch that can look very effective. It is best executed in a single, twisted thread such as perlé or coton à broder and it is beneficial to use a tapestry needle. You can use this stitch for daisies or asters, or any star-shaped flower.

1. Use a water soluble pen to draw a circle the size you want your spider's web to be. Bring the thread up at 12 o'clock, go down at 6 o'clock, up at 9 o'clock and back down at 3 o'clock to make an upright cross.

2. Make a diagonal cross across these stitches so that you have 8 equally spaced spokes across the circle. Come up near the centre of the circle and make a small holding stitch over the crossed threads in the middle.

3. You will now whip these spokes from the middle outwards. The thread will not go through the fabric again until the web has been completed. Come up near the centre to the left of a spoke and take your needle back over that spoke, pass the needle under it and forward under the next spoke.

4. Work your way around the circle by going back over one spoke and forward under two.

5. Keep going and the circle will gradually fill up as shown.

When the circle is full, take the thread to the back and finish off. Then, using a paintbrush and clean cold water, remove the blue line made by the water soluble pen.

Whipped spider's web with an open middle

This is similar to the previous stitch, but has a space in the middle that you can fill with French knots. As in the spider's web, you will be whipping the spokes from the middle outwards, using a single twisted thread and a tapestry needle.

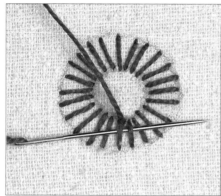

1. Draw two concentric circles and space the spokes evenly around between the two circles, leaving the middle empty. Come up near one of the spokes, back over that spoke and forward under two.

2. Continue like this, back over one and forwards under two, until the circle is complete and the spokes are covered.

The finished whipped spider's web with an open middle. The centre is filled with French knots to make a flower.

Raised chain band

This is a composite stitch, which means it is done in two parts. The thread for the first part of the stitch goes through the fabric, creating a ladder and the second part of the stitch is worked on this ladder without going through the fabric, except at the beginning and the end. I have used this stitch to create lupins and delphiniums but it can also be used to create a textured tree trunk. It is best executed in a single twisted thread such as perlé or coton à broder, using a tapestry needle. You can use a pointed needle when making the ladder, then change to a tapestry for the second part of the stitch.

  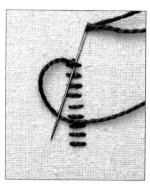 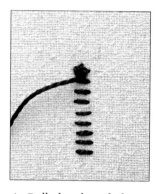

1. Make a ladder of small straight stitches as shown, then bring the thread to the front above and in the middle of the top rung.

2. Keep the thread to the right and pass the needle under the top rung from bottom to top and to the left of the thread.

3. Go back under the top rung from top to bottom on the right of the thread, making sure that the thread is under the needle.

4. Pull the thread down towards you to make a chain stitch on the rung. Continue all the way down the ladder, going up on the left and down on the right on every rung. Finish by going down through to the back of the fabric under the last rung.

The finished row of raised chain band stitch.

Note

If you do all the rows in the same direction, the finished effect will be smooth. If you want a more textured effect, you can alternate the rows by going up with one row and down with the next.

Raised stem band

Raised stem band is another composite stitch, very much like raised chain band. A ladder is made in the same way, and this time you work rows of stem stitch on the ladder rather than rows of chain stitch. It is a less textured and smoother stitch and you can use it, among other things, to represent wooden panels (see the gate on page 1, the beams on page 49 and the breakwater on page 53). As with raised chain band, use a perlé or coton à broder thread and a tapestry needle. You can make the ladder using a pointed needle, then change to a tapestry needle to add the rows of stem stitch.

1. Make a ladder of small straight stitches of the desired width, then bring the thread through to the front of the fabric below the bottom rung and near the left-hand side.

2. Keeping the thread to the right, pass the needle from top to bottom under the bottom rung.

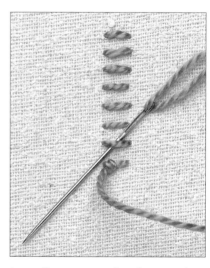

3. Pull to secure this first stitch then continue up each rung, keeping the thread to the right.

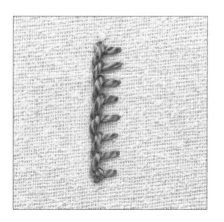

4. Continue until you reach the top of the ladder, then take the thread to the back of the fabric. Come back up at the bottom and do another row to the right of the first one. Sew as many rows as necessary to fill the ladder.

The finished raised stem band stitch.

Woven rose

This is a quick and easy way to create a small, raised rose, executed in two stages. First create a circle of spokes using perlé cotton, then weave on to these spokes using stranded cotton with all six strands pulled from the skein. You need an uneven number of spokes to weave on. Use a sharp needle when making the spokes, then change to a tapestry to weave the rose. I have used this stitch to make the roses on the left-hand side of the window on page 49.

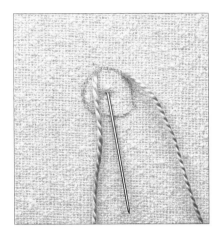

1. Use a water soluble pen to draw a circle the size you wish your finished rose to be. Bring the perlé thread through to the front of the fabric at 11 o'clock, and go down at 1 o'clock. Come up in the centre. Make sure the thread is under the needle.

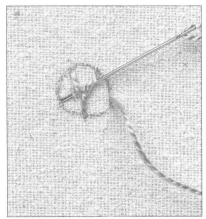

2. Go down at 6 o'clock to create a fly stitch (a Y shape). Come up on the outside of the circle, midway between two spokes and take the needle under the two top prongs of the Y. Go down on the outside of the circle, midway between the two spokes on the left hand side.

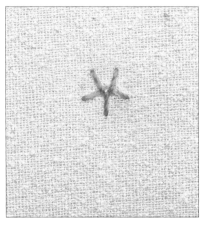

3. You should now have a wheel shape with five spokes. Secure with a small stitch in the backing fabric and finish off the thread. Erase the circle made with the water soluble pen by using a paint brush dipped in clean, cold water.

4. Thread the tapestry needle with the six strands of stranded cotton pulled straight from the skein. Come up in the middle and begin weaving anticlockwise, from the middle to the outside, over and under the spokes until all the spokes are filled. Take the thread to the back and finish off.

The finished woven rose.

Banksia rose

This is another stitch shown to me by Muriel Best, executed using six strands of stranded cotton straight from the skein. It is particularly lovely if you use a variegated thread so that the rose is darker in the middle and gradually gets lighter towards the outside. Great care must be taken not to pull the thread tightly so that the stitches become flat – each petal must rest on top of the one before giving a raised, soft look. This effect of overlapping petals will help to make the rose look realistic.

 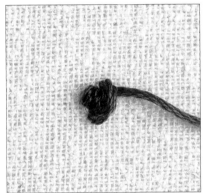 

1. Thread the needle with six strands of stranded cotton straight from the skein. Make three little loops (like croquet hoops) side by side very close to each other to create the tight centre of the rose. You could make them over a spare needle to get the loops the same size. These loops form the centre of the rose and must not be pulled flat. Secure with a small holding stitch so that the loops keep their shape. Come up close to the three stitches and go back down again, also very close.

2. Come up on the outside of the three loops and, working anticlockwise, go back down a third of the way round to make a larger loop than those in step 1. This is the first petal. Do not pull it tight, let it rest on the three original loops. Come up just behind where you went down.

3. Go down a third of the way around to make the second petal, letting it lie loosely, then come up behind where you went down and tuck the third petal round the back of the first petal. Keep going round, making overlapping petals. As the rose gets larger, if one stitch seems a long stretch, you can make two overlapping petals. When the rose is complete, finish off by making a small holding stitch in the backing fabric, so that the petals cannot be pulled flat.

The finished banksia rose

Raised leaf

This leaf is slightly raised from the surface and makes a very good leaf for a rose. I have also used it for leaves on sunflowers and hollyhocks. This stitch looks better if the threads are smooth, so it is made with four strands of stranded cotton which have been separated and put back together again. It is worked from the tip of the leaf to the stem over a piece of card. The width of the card will determine the width of the finished leaf, and how many stitches you work down the card will determine the length. Practise initially with a piece of card that is 4mm (³/₁₆in) wide, and later adjust the width where necessary to suit your design.

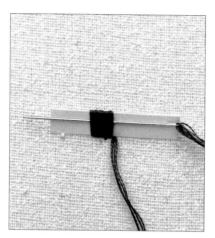

1. Hold the piece of card at right angles to the fabric so that it stands on its edge. Angle the card in the direction you want your leaf. Bring the thread to the front of the fabric, over the card and – for this first time only – go back down the same hole. This is important as it will give you a sharp point on your leaf. If you do not go back down the same hole, you will have a gap at the tip of the leaf.

2. Now work your way down the card, from the tip to the stem of your leaf, left to right. Come up again close to the first stitch on one side of the card, go over the card and go down again on the other side. The number of times you do this will determine the length of your leaf, I usually make about four or five stitches. Then bring the needle and thread to the front of the fabric and slide the needle between the card and the stitches from right to left, taking care not the split the threads.

3. Pull the thread all the way through, hold on to the stitches and gently withdraw the card from left to right. Take hold of the working thread and gently pull it over the stitches to the right so that they lay flat on the surface.

Take the thread through to the back. Make the stem the length you want it and finish off.

Bullion knot

This stitch looks like a wrapped bar and in the past has been known as 'worm stitch'. It is possible to vary the shape of the stitch to make curves and loops and this is how I created the flowers on pages 2–3. If you wrap the thread around the needle just enough times to fill the gap between the start and end of the stitch, it will be flat on the surface. If you leave a smaller gap but still make the same number of wraps, then the stitch cannot lie flat and will curve into a horseshoe shape. It is best executed using a single, twisted thread such as perlé, with a long darning needle or a long milliner's needle.

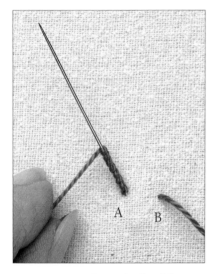

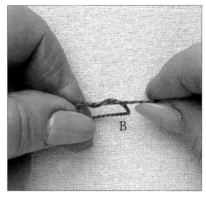

1. Come up through the fabric where you want the stitch to start (A), go back down to the right (B). The amount of space you leave between A and B will determine the length of the stitch. Take your needle to the back, but leave the thread in a loop at the front. Come up again at A in exactly the same hole, but do not bring the needle all the way through, hold on to the eye at the back of the fabric. Wrap the thread nearest the needle anticlockwise around it as many times as will fit the gap between A and B.

2. Hold on to the wraps with your left hand, and with your right hand pull the needle through to the front. Roll the stitches between your finger and thumb, towards you, to tighten them round the thread. Pull the working thread with your right hand and roll with your left.

3. Keep pulling the thread through until all the slack has been taken up and the stitch lies flat on the surface. Take the thread to the back through B.

You can vary this stitch by changing the amount of fabric you leave between A and B. In all the stitches on the right I have used perlé number 5. The top stitch was made over a 1cm (³∕₈in) gap with twelve wraps. The two other stitches used the same number of wraps but I reduced the gap – you can see that this makes the stitch curl.

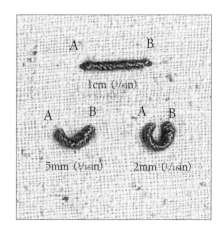

Cast on buttonhole

This stitch is similar to bullion knot, but instead of being smooth it has a raised edge. It is best executed in a single twisted thread such as perlé, using a milliner's needle. Like a bullion knot it is made on the needle, but instead of wrapping, you 'cast on'. You can vary the size and shape of the stitch, again like bullion knot, by varying the space between each end. This stitch was made using perlé 5 over a gap of 1cm (³/₈in) with fourteen cast on stitches.

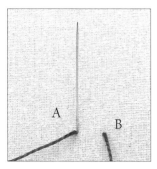

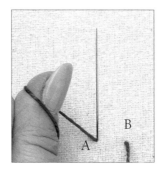

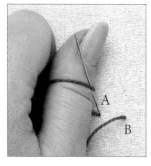

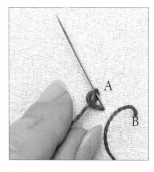

1. Come up at A and go down at B, leaving a gap the length you want your stitch to be. Do not pull all the thread through, leave a loop at the front. Come back up at A, in the same hole, but do not pull the whole needle through. Hold on to the eye of the needle at the back with your right hand.

2. Put the thread to the left of A and grip it in the palm of your left hand, leaving your thumb free. Place your thumb on the thread and rotate your thumb towards you so the thread goes round your thumb as shown.

3. Pass the point of the needle under the thread upwards from the base to the tip of your thumb.

4. Now remove your thumb so that the loop is cast on to the needle. Pull the thread so that it is snug on the needle, but not too tight.

5. Cast on as many stitches as you need to fill the space between A and B. You can check that you have cast on the right number by laying the needle down in the gap as shown. Hold on to the stitches and pull the needle through to the front of the fabric.

6. Ease the stitches off the needle. Keep pulling the thread until all the slack has been taken up and the stitch lies flat on the surface of the fabric. Take the needle to the back at B using the same hole and finish off.

Both of the two curled buttonholes here have fourteen cast on stitches. The wave has twenty cast on stitches over a 1cm (³/₈in) gap which is six more stitches than a 1cm gap usually needs. The extra cast ons make the stitch crinkle into a wave. All three examples use perlé number 5.

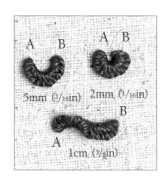

5mm (³/₁₆in)   2mm (¹/₁₆in)

1cm (³/₈in)

Velvet stitch

Velvet stitch is a canvas work stitch. It is usually worked on canvas because it is based on a square and canvas lends itself well to this shape, but it can also be done on fabric if you mark out the square grid. The stitch is made with loops held down by a cross stitch; the loops are then cut, resulting in a velvet pile. It is best to use threads that will fluff up easily when cut, such as stranded cotton or tapestry wool, and you can use multiples of thread in the needle at the same time. Start with the bottom row and work upwards across the grid, so that the loops of the second row lie on top of the first row and so on. I have used this stitch to represent the grass in front of the stone wall on page 1.

1. Using a blue water soluble pen, mark out a square grid to cover your design. I have used nine squares in the sample above. Work from left to right beginning at the bottom row. Come up in the bottom left-hand corner of the first square and go down in the top right-hand corner, making a flat diagonal stitch.

2. Come up again in the bottom left-hand corner and go down in the top right hand corner, but this time leave a small loop of thread on the surface. Hold this in place with your left thumb.

3. Come up in the bottom right-hand corner of the small square and go down in the top left hand corner. This stitch holds the loop in place.

4. Come up again in the bottom right-hand corner of the first square and you are ready to repeat steps 1–3 in the adjoining square.

5. Complete the bottom row of squares, then go to the left-hand side of the middle row and using the holes along the top of the first row, work the middle row. Do not leave a gap between rows. Then work the top row using the holes along the top of the middle row. I have used a space-dyed thread to produce a variety of colours.

6. When you have covered the whole area, cut the loops using a sharp pair of embroidery scissors and trim the threads to the height you want.

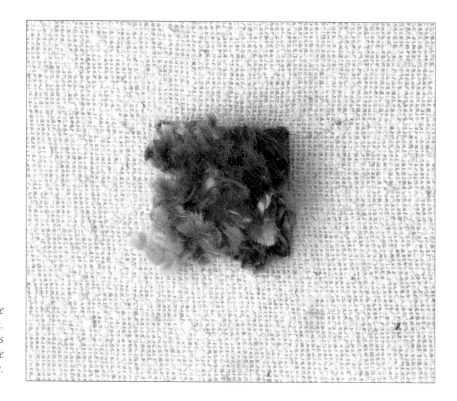

When all the loops are cut, the square has the look of velvet. You can brush the threads with a toothbrush to make them fluffy.

Other techniques

Rocks

Over the next four pages, I am going to explain a few techniques which, although not strictly stitches, can be used in conjunction with stitches to produce some lovely effects. The first is a very easy way to produce rocks for a rockery using tight or stocking nylon and wadding. You can make rocks in a variety of colours depending on which colour stockings you use.

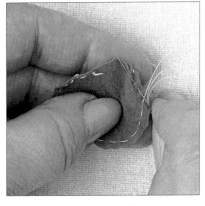

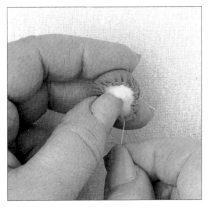

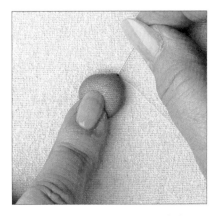

1. Cut a small circle from stocking nylon. Using a betweens needle threaded with sewing cotton with a knot in the end, sew a row of small running stitches around the edge of the circle.

2. Place a piece of wadding on the circle, and pull up the running stitches so that the stocking nylon encloses the wadding.

3. Draw the stitches up tightly, then take the thread through the background fabric in the place where you want the rock to be. Catch the rock down all the way round with small stab stitches to hold it in place.

Three finished rocks. Placed close together they make a lovely rockery. To produce a flatter effect, which can be used for crazy paving or a stone wall, cover shapes cut from craft vilene (as shown on page 10) with stocking nylon.

Couching moss between rocks

Couching with a textured thread is a quick and easy way to produce the effect of moss, or flowers, growing in between rocks or stones. You can also use couching in combination with French knots.

In this sample I have used a bouclé thread for the moss and one strand of stranded cotton to make the couching stitches. Lay the textured thread where you want the moss to be and using a fine needle threaded with a fine thread, come up from the back. Gather the bouclé thread and couch it down in a lump to look like moss.

The moss was made with a green bouclé thread. If you use a space-dyed or variegated thread, it can be used to represent flowers – see the left hand side of these rocks.

Pebbles

The method I described for making rocks also produces boulders, but I use a different technique for pebbles so that I can vary the height, shape and colour. The pebbles are made with stocking nylon which is very stretchy, so you can stuff it with as little or as much filling as you wish, producing pebbles of differing heights.

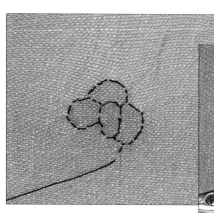

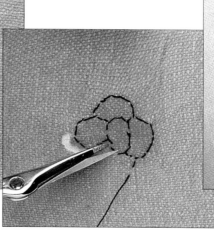

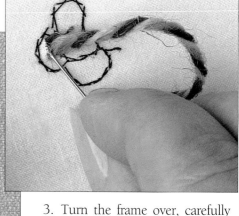

1. Stretch the stocking nylon over the background fabric tightly on a tambour frame. Using sewing cotton, sew the shapes of the pebbles using back stitch as shown.

2. Use embroidery scissors to carefully cut round the pebble shapes, cutting the stocking fabric only. It will spring back from the sewn pebble shapes because it was stretched tightly. Take the stocking nylon off the frame and put the background fabric back in the frame.

3. Turn the frame over, carefully cut a slit in the background fabric within the pebble shape and stuff in some textured thread using the blunt eye of the needle.

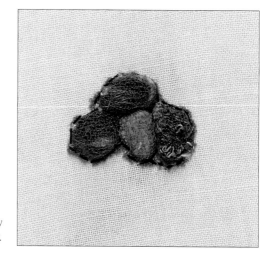

The finished pebbles using a variety of different threads for the stuffing.

Twisted thread tree trunk

This is a very quick and easy way to make a tree trunk. If you have a bundle of textured threads that are difficult to pass through fabric without shredding, you can twist them together and couch them down. I have used this technique to create the tree trunk on page 1.

 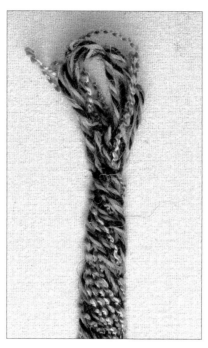 

1. Twist thick, textured threads together and lay them on the fabric. Couch them down using a fine needle and a fine, matching thread such as one strand of stranded cotton. Try to hide your couching stitches in the twist of the textured threads.

2. When you have couched up to the top of the trunk, divide the threads to make the branches.

3. Twist and couch sections of the thread to create each branch. Then twist even smaller and thinner sections to make twigs. Keep dividing the threads to create the effect you want.

Sampler

All the flowers in this sampler have been made using the stitches described in this book. There are many more possibilities than we have room to show you. Combining stitches and colours in different ways will produce many other flowers. Have fun trying out the stitches to create the flowers you wish to have in your garden scene.

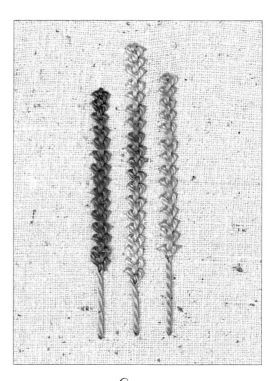

Lupins
Stems: stem stitch
Flowers: one row of raised chain band

Sunflower
Stem: Portuguese knotted stem
Petals: woven picots
Centre: French knots
Leaves: raised leaf

Asters
Stems: stem stitch
Flowers: whipped spider's web

Hollyhock

Stem: Portuguese knotted stem

Flower, from top: French knots in green, French knots in purple, then a series of raised cups with a French knot in yellow at each centre

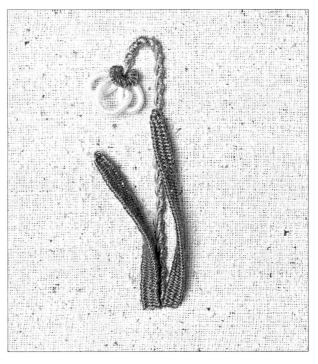

Snowdrop

Stem: Portuguese knotted stem
Petals: long curved bullion knots
Cap: curved cast on buttonhole
Leaves: long woven picots

Daisies

Stems: stem stitch

Flowers: flat bullion knots (top and two at bottom), bullion knots with a few extra wraps to make them stand up in a little hump (right and left)
Work the bullions at North, South, East and West first, then fit in the other bullions equally in between.

Corn and Lavender

Stems: stem stitch
Corn: bullion knots
Lavender: bullion knots

Bell-shaped flower

Stem: Portuguese knotted stem

Leaves: woven picots

Petals: frilly cast on buttonholes

Work the middle petal first as it is the longest. Then work the two petals on either side, making them a little shorter, then two outside petals, a little shorter again.

Pom Pom Chrysanthemum

Stem: Portuguese knotted stem

Petals: frilly cast on buttonhole

Centre: French knots

Leaves: raised leaf

Work the petals at North, South, West and East first, then fit in the others equally between them at regular intervals until full.

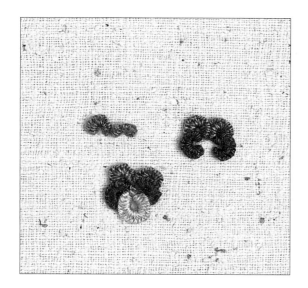

Pansy

Curved cast on buttonhole, shown in stages so that you can see where to place each petal.

Work the top two petals first, make fourteen cast on stitches over a 2mm (¹/₁₆in) gap using perlé 8. Then work the side petals with seventeen cast on stitches, followed by the bottom petal with twenty-three cast on stitches. The middle is a French knot.

Roses

Stem: Palestrina knot
Left-hand rose: overlapping frilly buttonholes
Centre rose: long curved bullion knots
Right-hand rose: flat bullion knots
Leaves: raised leaf

Daffodil

Stem: stem stitch
Petals: woven picots
Trumpet: raised cup stitch
Leaves: woven picots

Delphiniums

Stem: stem stitch
Flower: three rows of raised chain band

How to start

Framing

I like to work on a frame that is large enough for me to see the whole of my design at once. Working on a frame keeps the fabric taut and under tension in both directions, ensuring that the fabric is drum tight. I work on a home-made square or rectangular frame and the following steps show you how to dress a similar frame. I use silk noil as the top background fabric, and a fine calico as a backing fabric. I stretch both of these fabrics at the same time.

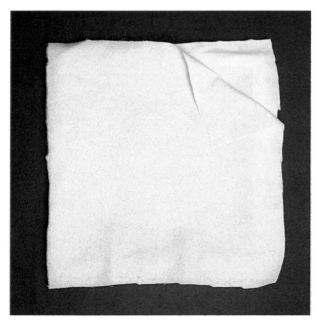

1. Put the square of silk noil on top of the square of fine calico and place both fabrics over the frame. Position the fabrics centrally on the frame so that there is an equal amount of overhanging fabric along each edge.

2. Using a staple gun, staple the fabric in place. Staple the right-hand side first, working from the middle outwards to each corner. Then pull the fabric very taut and staple the left-hand side in the same way. Repeat along the top and bottom keeping the fabric as taut as possible. You must staple in this sequence, because if you start at one corner and work your way around the frame, the fabric might pucker and will not be drum tight. If you do not have a staple gun, drawing pins or silk pins can be used, but keep to the same sequence.

Colouring fabric

There are countless ways to colour fabric but using water soluble pencils or crayons is one of the simplest. Many people feel more comfortable using a pencil or crayon than a brush so these techniques are especially good when you are first experimenting with colour. However, they are not colour-fast and obviously should only be used on a piece of embroidery that you do not intend to wash.

Water soluble crayons on dry fabric

1. Apply the water soluble crayon dry, on dry fabric. You can see that this produces a soft, light colour.

2. Using a paint brush dipped in cold water, wet the crayon marks and they will darken and spread like water-colour paint.

Water soluble crayons on wet fabric

1. Rub the water soluble crayon on to wet fabric. You can see that the colour is denser than when it is used on dry fabric.

2. Add another colour and blend the two colours together using a brush that you have wet with clean water.

Note

You can also dab a wet brush on to a water soluble crayon to pick up colour and then paint straight on to dry fabric.

Fabric paints

If you are confident with a brush, then you can apply your colour wash using fabric paints. Once they are dry, you simply iron the fabric to fix the colours permanently. Please read the manufacturers' instructions on the side of the bottle to see how to do this.

Dilute the fabric paint with cold water and apply with a brush. You can see that the colour is very intense and that it spreads easily giving a lovely, even wash.

Here fabric paint is applied with a sponge. This method will give a more textured look.

Threading a needle

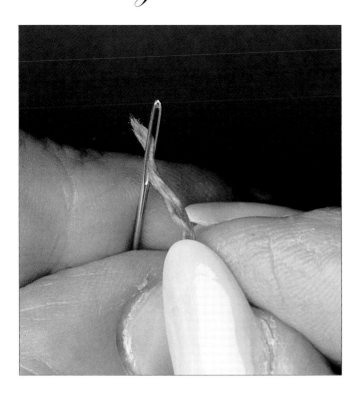

Thread is round but the eye of a needle is flat, so I usually flatten the thread between my teeth so that I can push it through easily, as shown.

Beginning and ending threads

I begin and end my threads in the backing fabric to be sure that the stitches I make do not show through at the front and spoil my picture.

1. Make a small stitch in the backing fabric as shown.

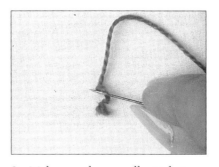

2. Make another small stitch in the same place. When you pull the thread through, leave a small loop and pass the needle and thread under this loop.

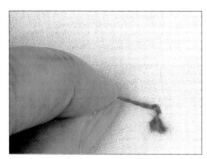

3. Pull the thread through and it will tighten into a knot, then go through to the front of the fabric. You finish the thread off in exactly the same way.

Rockery Garden

When embroidering it is best to think in layers and work upwards from the fabric. For instance, it is much easier to embroider a flower on top of a stem than to stitch a stem under a flower. This design is a good example of building up texture. It was worked on silk noil with a fine calico backing. I stretched the fabrics on to the frame, then I painted a coloured wash for the sky, meadow and pond. The finished embroidery measures 25.4 x 20.3cm (10 x 8in).

You will need

Rectangular home-made frame, 28 x 23cm (11 x 9in)
Silk noil, 33 x 28cm (13 x 11in)
Fine calico, 33 x 28cm (13 x 11in)
Staple gun and staples
Water soluble marker pen, blue
Water soluble crayons: blue, grey, light green, dark green
Paint brush
Stocking or tight nylon, 15.3 x 15.3cm (6 x 6in)
Betweens needle, size 10
Chenille needles, sizes 18 and 22
Long doll needle
Long milliner's needle, size 3
Tapestry needle, size 24
Glass-headed pin
Sewing cotton
Wadding
Craft vilene
Embroidery scissors
Coton à broder, green
Boucle yarn, green and space-dyed
Perlé 3 in green and brown
Perlé 5 in green and brown
Perlé 8 in red, orange, yellow and green
Stranded cotton in brown, white, yellow, pale pink, fuchsia pink

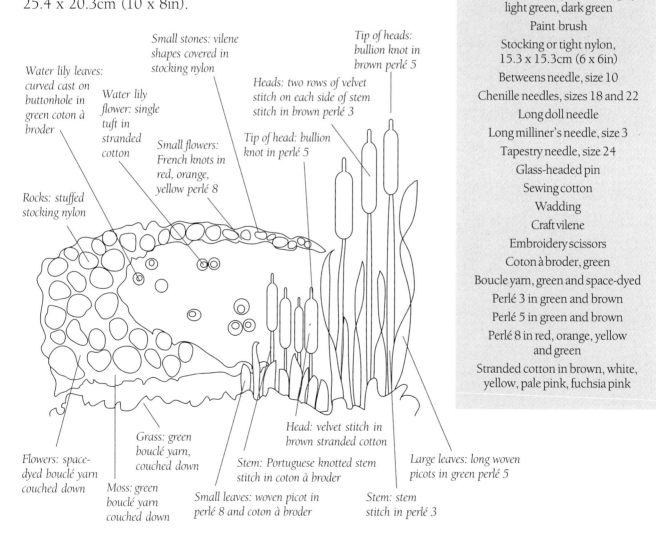

Small stones: vilene shapes covered in stocking nylon

Tip of heads: bullion knot in brown perlé 5

Heads: two rows of velvet stitch on each side of stem stitch in brown perlé 3

Water lily leaves: curved cast on buttonhole in green coton à broder

Water lily flower: single tuft in stranded cotton

Small flowers: French knots in red, orange, yellow perlé 8

Tip of head: bullion knot in perlé 5

Rocks: stuffed stocking nylon

Flowers: space-dyed bouclé yarn couched down

Grass: green bouclé yarn, couched down

Moss: green bouclé yarn couched down

Small leaves: woven picot in perlé 8 and coton à broder

Stem: Portuguese knotted stem stitch in coton à broder

Head: velvet stitch in brown stranded cotton

Stem: stem stitch in perlé 3

Large leaves: long woven picots in green perlé 5

2. These bulrushes were executed in stages to show the order of work. Mark them out with a blue marker pen. Use a chenille needle to embroider each stem (see stem stitch, page 14), and work a line of stem stitch up the middle of the head. Add two rows of velvet stitch (see page 30) on each side. Use a milliner's needle to add a bullion knot (see page 28) to the tip and then cut the loops of the velvet stitch.

1. Stretch the two fabrics, silk noil with a fine calico backing, on to a frame using a staple gun. Apply a colour wash, dry on dry, using water soluble crayons. Divide the fabric roughly into one third sky and two thirds garden green, with the pond area in blue and the rockery area in grey. When you have applied all the colours, use a clean brush dipped in water to blend them.

3. Work the bulrush leaves in long woven picot stitch (see page 19). When making spokes, use the long doll needle for the tallest leaves and the glass-headed pin for the others. Weave on to the spokes using a tapestry needle. Twist each leaf and make small stitches at intervals along its length using a fine needle and one strand of stranded cotton or sewing cotton. These small stitches will stop the leaf from falling forward. You can leave the smaller ones completely free of the fabric at the top, just attached at the bottom where they are worked. Work the stems of the smaller bulrushes (*not shown*) in Portuguese knotted stem stitch using coton à broder.

4. Mark out where you want the rockery to be and attach the rocks using the technique described on page 32.

5. Couch green moss between the rocks (see page 33) using a betweens needle threaded with one strand of stranded cotton or sewing cotton.

6. Use the same technique to add flowers but this time couch down space-dyed bouclé.

7. The top right-hand section of the rockery was made with small, shaped pieces of vilene, each enclosed in a circle of stocking nylon and sewn in place. Work small French knots with a chenille needle in between the rocks to represent flowers. Add the water lilies in curved cast on button hole stitch (see page 29) in green, using a milliner's needle. Add a small tufting stitch (see page 18) to the centre of each water lily. Couch green bouclé using a betweens needle threaded with one strand of stranded cotton or sewing cotton along the bottom of the picture for grass.

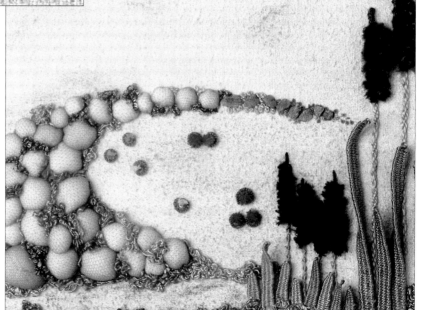

Roses are Red

Most people love the idea of a country cottage with roses round the door. Whilst this project is not quite that, it does feature roses round the window. Mark out the beams and work them first, then embroider the stems around the window and over the beams. Finally, add the roses and leaves. The finished embroidery measures 20.3 x 25.4cm (8 x 10in).

You will need

Rectangular home-made frame, 23 x 28cm (11 x 9in)

Silk noil, 28 x 33cm (11 x 13in)

Fine calico, 28 x 33cm (11 x 13in)

Staple gun and staples

Water soluble marker pen, blue

Water soluble crayon, grey

Perlé 3 in light green, olive green and brown

Perlé 5 in light green, olive green and brown

Perlé 8 in red

Stranded cotton in red and variegated red/yellow

Stranded cotton, green

Chenille needle size 22

Tapestry needle size 24

Embroidery scissors

Small piece of card for leaves

Roses: woven rose stitch in red stranded cotton

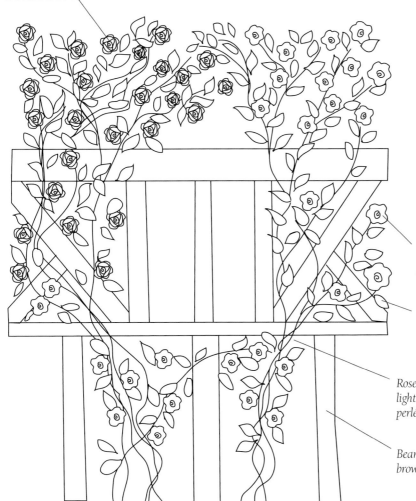

Roses: Banksia rose in variegated red/yellow stranded cotton

Leaves: raised leaf stitch in stranded cotton

Rose stems: Palestrina knot in light green and olive green in both perlé 3 and perlé 5

Beams: raised stem band in brown perlé 3

48

1. Use silk noil as the top fabric and fine calico for the backing fabric. Stretch them on to the frame using a staple gun. Mark out the beams with a blue water soluble marker pen, then shade in the window area with a water soluble crayon.

2. Embroider the beams using raised stem band (see page 24). Make ladders using a chenille needle and perlé 3 first, then work stem stitch with a tapestry needle and brown perlé 5 on to the ladders.

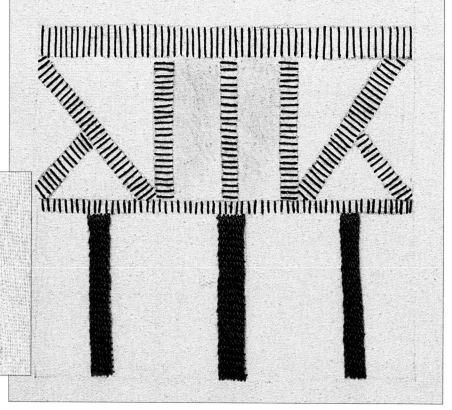

3. When you have completed the beams, mark out the rose stems with a blue water soluble marker pen. Now embroider the stems in Palestrina knot stitch (see page 15) in two shades of green using a chenille needle. Use perlé 3 for most of the stem, changing to perlé 5 as it becomes finer.

4. Following the pattern on page 48, now add roses. Work the woven roses (see page 25) with six strands of stranded cotton in red on to spokes stitched in perlé 8. Use a chenille needle to make the spokes and weave the rose with a tapestry needle. Work the banksia roses (see page 26) with a chenille needle and six strands of stranded cotton in a variegated thread of red/yellow. Use raised leaf stitch (see page 27) to make leaves with a chenille needle, a small piece of card and four strands of stranded cotton in green.

Beach at Dusk

After embroidering so many flowers, I thought it would make a
nice change to embroider a tranquil seaside scene. It reminds me
of the beach when everyone has gone home after a lovely day out.
The finished embroidery measures 17.8 x 17.8cm (7 x 7in).

You will need

Square home-made frame,
23 x 23cm (9 x 9in)

Silk noil, 28 x 28cm (11 x 11in)

Fine calico, 28 x 28cm (11 x 11in)

Staple gun and staples

Blue water soluble marker pen

Water soluble crayons in blue,
pink, yellow, orange and brown

Paint brush

Stocking or tight nylon

Sewing cotton

Different coloured textured threads
for stuffing pebbles

Betweens needle size 10

Chenille needle size 22

Tapestry needle size 24

Perlé 5 in light, mid and dark
brown

Embroidery scissors

*Breakwater: raised stem band stitch
in perlé 5 in two different browns*

*Small pebbles: French
knots in perlé 5 in light,
mid and dark brown*

*Pebbles: stocking nylon stuffed with
different coloured textured threads*

52

1. Stretch silk noil and fine calico over the frame using a staple gun. Use water soluble crayons to colour the areas of sky, sand, sea and a small rock pool. Apply the crayons on dry fabric and then brush over the coloured areas with a wet paint brush.

2. Stretch stocking nylon over the areas where you want the pebbles and then work back stitch around them. Cut away the excess stocking nylon (see page 34).

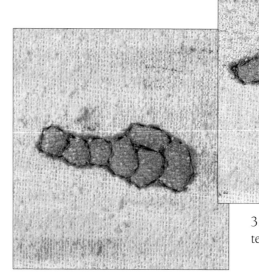

3. Stuff each of the pebbles with textured thread (see page 34).

4. Draw in the breakwater using a blue water soluble marker pen. Use a chenille needle to work a ladder over each section of breakwater. This is the first stage of raised stem band stitch (see page 24).

5. With a tapestry needle, start to work the breakwater in raised stem band stitch. Begin with the uprights and then weave the horizontal planks.

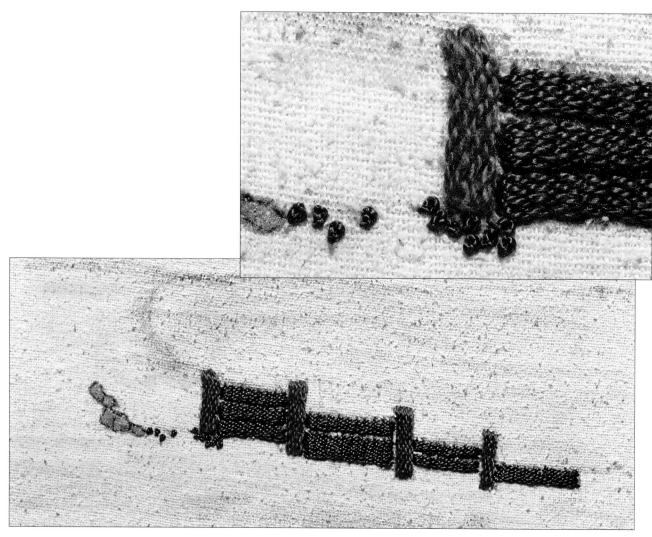

6. Now add French knots (see page 17) with a
chenille needle in perlé 5 to represent small stones
and pebbles around the bottom of the breakwater.

7. Create more pebbles following the diagram on page 52. Add French knots where smaller pebbles are needed.

Daffodil Wood

Daffodils are cheerful flowers that herald the arrival of Spring, so they are always a welcome sight. They look beautiful *en masse*, so I thought I would stitch a carpet of daffodils in a wood. When working the daffodils, tackle the petals first, then do raised cups for the trumpets. If you do the trumpet first, it will get in the way when you try to make the petals. Be warned – this design needs lots of flowers and leaves and takes a long time to complete, but it is worth the effort. The finished embroidery measures 20.3 x 25.4cm (8 x 10in).

You will need

Rectangular home-made frame, 22.8 x 28cm (9 x 11in)

Silk noil, 28 x 33cm (11 x 13in)

Fine calico, 28 x 33cm (11 x 13in)

Staple gun and staples

Blue water soluble marker pen

Water soluble crayons in blue and green

Textured threads such as chenille and bouclé in browns and greens

Perlé 3 in brown
Perlé 5 in green

Perlé 8 in yellow, white, orange and green

Coton à broder in yellow, white and green

Stranded cotton in yellow

Chenille needle size 22

Tapestry needles size 24 and 26

Embroidery scissors

Glass-headed pin

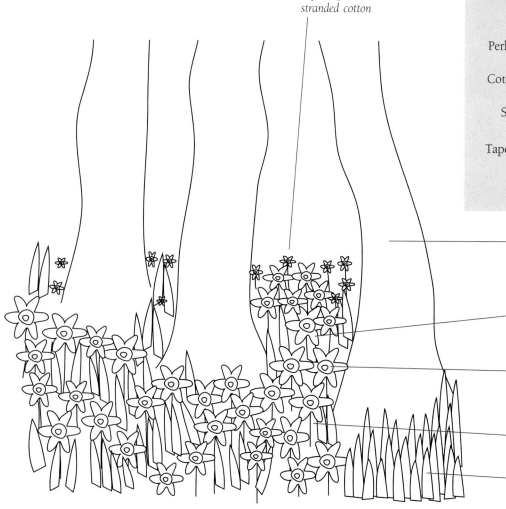

Tufts in yellow stranded cotton

Trees: raised chain band in chenille, bouclé and hollow ribbon yarn in greens and browns. Ladder in perlé 3

Daffodil petals: woven picot in perlé 8 and coton à broder in yellow, white and orange

Daffodil trumpets: raised cup stitch in perlé 8 and coton à broder

Daffodil stems: stem stitch in green perlé 5

Leaves: woven picot in green perlé 5 and perlé 8

58

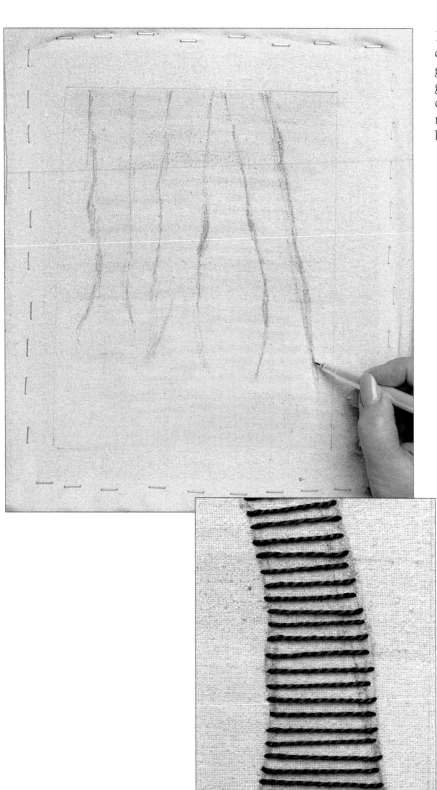

1. Stretch your silk noil and fine calico on to a frame using a staple gun. Then apply the sky and grass areas with water soluble crayons in blue and green. Next mark out the tree trunks with a blue water soluble marker pen.

2. The tree trunks will all be embroidered in raised chain band. With a chenille needle and perlé 3 in brown, work a ladder across each tree trunk.

3. With a tapestry needle and using a mixture of textured threads in a combination of different browns and greens, build up the raised chain band stitches (see page 23) on the first trunk.

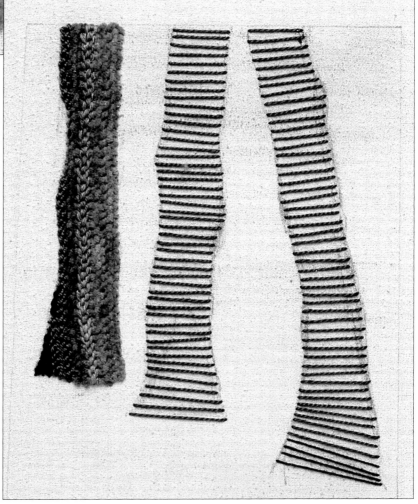

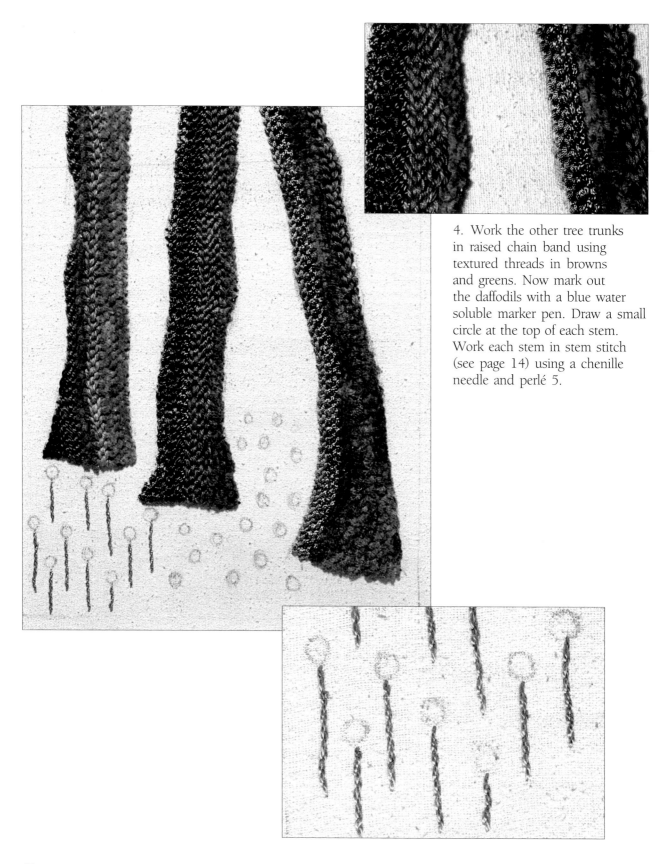

4. Work the other tree trunks in raised chain band using textured threads in browns and greens. Now mark out the daffodils with a blue water soluble marker pen. Draw a small circle at the top of each stem. Work each stem in stem stitch (see page 14) using a chenille needle and perlé 5.

5. Work the daffodil petals in woven picots (see page 19) using perlé 8 and coton à broder in a mixture of yellows, orange and white. Make the spokes with a chenille needle and weave the petals with a tapestry needle. Next work the daffodil trumpets in raised cup stitch (see page 20) with a tapestry needle. Add the leaves in longer woven picots in between the flowers wherever they fit. Use perlé 5 for the larger leaves and perlé 8 for the smaller ones. The smallest daffodils at the back are tufts (see page 18) made with stranded cotton.

Index